Myth Quest
Nandi
THE DIVINE GATEKEEPER

retold by Anu Kumar

illustrations by Maya Magical Studios

First published in 2011 by Hachette India
An Hachette UK company

www.hachetteindia.com

SRD

ISBN: 978-93-5009-285-9

Hachette India
612/614 (6th Floor), Time Tower
MG Road, Sector 28, Gurgaon 122001, India

Typeset in Adobe Garamond Pro 13/16 by
Eleven Arts, New Delhi

Printed and bound in India by
Manipal Technologies Limited, Manipal

MIX
Paper | Supporting responsible forestry
FSC™ C043100

Welcome to the world of MythQuest…

Discover the fables and legends about the origin, history, deities, ancestors and heroes of India.

While the term 'myth' in common conversation means a false story, in the world of religion, folklore and magic, myths are considered 'true'. They tell stories of the creation of the universe, the eternal battle between good and evil, and the history of humankind itself.

The main characters in our myths are bigger and better than any modern superheroes. They are birds and beasts, gods and demons, kings and queens, generals and warriors, sages and gurus, each with extraordinary powers that changed the course of history and the fate of the human race.

The people to whom a myth belongs consider it a true account of their past millions of years ago. Even today, they continue to worship the gods and goddesses, follow the rituals and read the texts that developed from these myths.

Hachette's MythQuest series brings to you fascinating stories from the vast treasures of ancient mythology. Read them all—and become a MythMaster!

Mythological characters and events have been described in different ways in different versions of ancient texts. We have chosen the most interesting and key stories to build a comprehensive account for the young reader.

This story is about . . .

. . . Nandi, the white bull who was the dalapati *or the head of all of Shiva's followers or* ganas. *Some Puranas describe Nandi as Nandikeshvara—a creature with the head of a bull and the body of a human. Stories of Nandi's origin are varied. One story describes Nandi as the son of the sage Kashyapa and the divine cow Surabhi. In another story, Nandi is said to have emerged from the right side of Lord Vishnu, the Preserver of the Universe, and resembled Shiva—then he was given by Vishnu to the sage Salankayana. According to the Shiva Purana, Nandi was born to the sage Shilada after he was blessed by Shiva. In addition to the Shiva Purana, Nandi is mentioned in the Nilamata Purana, the Nandi Purana and the Linga Purana.*

Nandi was Shiva's vahana *or vehicle as well as his gatekeeper. That's why one often finds a Nandi statue at the entrance of many Shiva temples. He also accompanied Shiva in great battles and danced in rhythm to Lord Shiva's* tandava*—the dance of creation, preservation and dissolution.*

Nandi was brave, knowledgeable and ever obedient to Shiva. Often considered as another form of Lord Shiva himself, Nandi is also worshipped as the God of Joy. This divine bull is regarded as a symbol of energy and fertility. His white colour represents purity.

Here is Nandi's story, full of battle cries and the rhythms of Shiva's cosmic dance.

CHAPTER ONE

LORD SHIVA'S BOON

The sage Shilada was righteous and very learned in all the sacred texts. However, he was childless and longed for a son to whom he could pass on his knowledge. So he began to pray to his beloved god, Shiva, meditating and chanting his name for more than a thousand years. Finally, Shiva, pleased with his devotee's efforts, chose to appear before him.

Shilada bowed before Shiva and said, 'Please grant me a boon so that I may have an immortal son who will not be born of any woman.'

Shiva blessed him and left. A little while later, as Shilada was ploughing his little plot of land, a handsome boy appeared on the edge of his plough. He radiated beauty and called the sage his father. Shilada named him Nandi—one who brings joy—and taught him all the *shastras* or religious scriptures. The boy soon rivalled his father's wisdom and also became a devotee of Shiva.

When Nandi was seven years old, two sages—Mitra and Varuna—visited his father's hermitage. They blessed the young boy, but they also told Shilada that his son would die in a year. Shilada was terribly upset and Nandi tried to comfort him.

Nandi expressed his desire to come face to face with his Lord and ask him for a boon that would extend his life. His father granted him his wish by teaching him the

mantras of worship. Thus Nandi went off to the seashore to meditate. He chanted the verses taught by his father more than a million times till Shiva finally appeared to grant Nandi a boon. Nandi responded saying, 'Please give me a life long enough to chant these verses in your honour a million times more.'

Nandi's boon was granted and when he had recited the mantras a million times again, Shiva reappeared and Nandi made the same request. When this happened three more times, Shiva was so pleased with his devotee's dedication that he said, 'There is really no more need for penance. Not only are you immortal now, you are also a *ganapati* or lord of the *ganas*. From now on, you will be my constant companion.' The blessing transformed Nandi into a divine creature and he then followed Lord Shiva to his abode at Mount Kailash.

Some Puranas tell the story that Nandi was originally the gatekeeper and *ganapati* of Shiva. But he was cursed by the sage Bhrigu, as a result of which he was born as a human child to Shilada. Even Shiva could not do anything as Bhrigu was a powerful sage. However, once Nandi had taken on his human form, thereby fulfilling the curse, Shiva could step in. Thus, when Nandi started praying to Shiva, he granted him a long life and restored Nandi to his position as *ganapati*, gatekeeper and *vahana*. Shiva also arranged for Nandi to be married to Suyasha, the daughter of the Wind God, Vayu.

Nandi was Shiva's constant companion, following

him and watching out for him. Shiva spent long periods of time in meditation. He would meditate for days and sometimes even years on end, sitting cross-legged in a yogic posture, with his eyes closed in deep concentration. This was when Nandi stood guard at the gate, letting no one inside.

However, there were also occasions when Shiva would

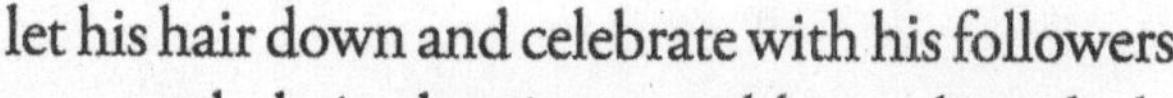

let his hair down and celebrate with his followers and their dancing would set the whole universe abuzz. He danced almost every cosmic evening. On such occasions, Nandi accompanied Shiva as he danced the *tandava*. Nandi received the first lessons in dancing from Lord Shiva himself.

All the gods either took part in this dancing or would at least witness it as it was a great honour to see Shiva dance. Lord Brahma, the Creator of the Universe, provided the *taal* or rhythm, Lord Vishnu would play the *mridanga* or the drum, Saraswati, the Goddess of Learning, would strum on the *veena*, the Moon God Soma would play the flute, Lord Narada, the Divine Sage, played the *tanpura*—a kind of lute—and sang, and the *apsaras* or heavenly nymphs would dance.

Apart from being Shiva's companion, Nandi also protected and accompanied Shiva's wives mostly everywhere he could—because who knew when evil might befall them?

CHAPTER TWO

A TERRIBLE SACRIFICE

Nandi was devoted to Sati—Shiva's beloved wife and consort. She was the daughter of Daksha, Brahma's son and the great *prajapati* or king of the people. She married Shiva after she had impressed him with her devotion and the two of them lived in perfect happiness.

Daksha was very proud and did not like Shiva. Furthermore, he was offended at his son-in-law's refusal to bow before him at a public gathering, unaware that Shiva, as a superior being, could not bow to anyone below him in the hierarchy. Despite being Brahma's son, Daksha was lower in status to Shiva. This humiliation fuelled his anger at his daughter who had gone against his wishes and married Shiva.

He decided to hold a great *yagna* or sacrificial fire, and invited all the gods except Sati and Shiva. When Sati heard about this *yagna*, she made her way there despite not being invited. Riding on Nandi, she entered her father's home only to be insulted by him. Even worse, Daksha insulted her husband—this upset Sati to such an extent that she immolated herself in the sacrificial fire after vowing to return to earth only when she was reborn to a better father.

Her sacrifice created a great stir among Nandi and the other *gana*s who were accompanying her. They immediately attacked Daksha, but were repelled by powerful demons released by the sage Bhrigu.

When Shiva heard about this, he was furious. He sent Virabhadra and Bhadrakali—super-beings created from the nebula of Shiva's anger—along with Nandi and the other *gana*s to kill Daksha.

Shiva's army attacked Daksha's army of demons and gods led by Indra, the Lord of Heaven and the God of War, himself. In the fierce battle which ensued, Indra was struck by Nandi's trident and in return he felled Nandi with his thunderbolt. When Virabhadra saw Shiva's favourite follower lying on the ground, he was enraged. He immediately attacked Indra and defeated him. Virabhadra's strength was unmatched and he ended the battle by chopping off Daksha's head.

However, after Vishnu and Brahma appealed to Shiva, he restored the *prajapati's* life by fixing a goat's head onto his neck. Daksha begged Shiva's forgiveness for his foolish pride.

After some time had passed, all those who had fallen in battle also returned to life. Nandi, Shiva's valiant warrior and mount, returned to Mount Kailash and continued to fulfil his duties to his lord.

CHAPTER THREE

THE END OF TWO ASURAS

One wouldn't think that Shiva's family would need any protection, but strange were the ways of Heaven. It was at such times of danger and distress that Nandi proved his mettle time and again—and with legendary loyalty as he did against a demon called Tarakasura, who had performed the most difficult of penances to please Lord Brahma. When the Creator of the Universe finally appeared before him, the demon asked for two boons. First, he wanted to be the strongest of all living beings ever created by Brahma, and second, if he ever had to

die, it should be only at the hands of Shiva's son.

Shiva had just then lost his wife Sati, and his anger had wrought great destruction. Thereafter, he sat in meditation and seemed likely to continue in that state for years and years. No one believed that he would ever remarry.

However, time changes many things, and after a long time Shiva fell in love with and married Parvati, who was a reincarnation of Sati herself. They had a son called Kartikeya.

When Tarakasura came to know of the birth of Kartikeya, he was most alarmed. He knew he could not continue with his evil ways because it would not be long before the boon granted by Brahma would take effect and he would be killed by Shiva's son. So Tarakasura decided to hunt down Kartikeya and kill him first.

The young god was then being brought up by the six goddesses called the *kritikas*. Once again, it was the brave and loyal Nandi who did all he could to protect his master's child and throw the demon off track. With alacrity and speed, he carried Kartikeya off to Mount Kailash, where he knew the *asura* would never dare to appear. He also had his fellow *ganas* kill as many of Tarakasura's followers as they could in order to deplete his strength.

However, this was not the end of the battle.

When Kartikeya was older and heard about this vicious demon, he assembled an army of gods and set off in force to kill him. The six-headed Kartikeya rose on a magnificent peacock and sailed across the skies in an effulgence of colour. In a fierce duel watched by all the gods, Kartikeya finally killed Tarakasura—and Brahma's words came true.

This did not end the troubles. Tripurasura, the son of Tarakasura, followed in his father's ways and harassed the gods continually, snatching their properties and

possessions and even raiding their abodes. The gods, hoping to escape his tyranny, fled to the wild jungles and dark caves.

Despite this, Tripurasura continued to hound the gods. In desperation, they went to Brahma for help. But Brahma had also run out of ideas and he turned to Vishnu. Finally, it was decided that only Lord Shiva could kill Tripurasura. So all the gods made their way to Mount Kailash and waited for Shiva to complete his meditation. When Shiva finally opened his eyes, Indra explained the matter to him.

'We want your help in killing Tripurasura,' Indra said. 'He has made our lives miserable and even chased us out of our heavenly abode.'

On hearing of Tripurasura's heinous deeds, the frown on Shiva's forehead deepened. Picking up his trident and fixing his serpent garland around his neck, Shiva rose to look for the *asura*.

When he found Tripurasura, he demolished his palace with a single arrow. Then he cut off the demon's head in one fell swoop of his trident.

Once he had restored peace, Shiva began dancing the *tandava*. He was still very angry and his dance reflected all his pent-up anger and rage. It was on this occasion that Shiva taught the *tandava* dance to his dear follower, Nandi. Nandi became adept at following the rhythms of the cosmic dance, and that is why he is also known as Tandu—he who knows the *tandava*.

Nandi further spread knowledge of this dance form, teaching it to others. The sage called Bharat Muni once prepared a drama on Brahma's instructions named 'Tripur Daah' and performed it with his disciples at Mount Kailash in front of Lord Shiva. Shiva was happy after seeing the performance and asked Tandu to teach the *tandava* to Bharat Muni so that his drama would be complete in every aspect.

CHAPTER FOUR

THE LOYAL GATEKEEPER

Nandi was ever loyal to Shiva and later to his family as well. Shiva's consort Parvati sometimes resented his interference and thought he bumbled around their household a bit too much.

Parvati came to be regarded as Shiva's equal in every way and even occupied half his body. They lived with their son Kartikeya at Mount Kailash, but Shiva left his home for long stretches to go away and meditate. Sometimes, he was accompanied by his faithful

companion Nandi, while at other times, he left him in charge and went away alone.

Nandi was very protective of all of Shiva's family but everything came second to his unending devotion to Lord Shiva himself.

Soon after Parvati married Shiva, she found several things that were hard to get used to. Shiva was a god with strange ways, quite different from other gods. He meditated, sang, danced and lived an austere life all at the same time. On top of that, he also lived with a large group of assorted creatures including *bhoot-pret* or ghosts and ghouls, gathered from cremation sites, who didn't quite know how to behave themselves.

Shiva did not care about these matters and would often turn up at Mount Kailash with his unruly companions who would raise a fearful din and disturb the peaceful lives of Parvati and her companions. Sometimes, the *bhoot-pret* turned up on their own as well and would force their way in. Even Nandi could not refuse them admission as they were friends of Shiva.

One day, Nandi stood guard while Parvati rested in her chambers with strict orders that she should not be disturbed. Right then, Shiva returned to Mount Kailash and did not think twice before entering Parvati's quarters. Nandi, of course, would not dream of stopping Shiva, and so he walked in casually. As the other *ganas* watched in trepidation, waiting for Parvati's anger to descend on Nandi, the latter stood, looking downcast. He knew he had disobeyed the goddess, but in front of Shiva, Nandi was tongue-tied and unable to remember any of Parvati's instructions.

Of course, when Parvati learnt of what had happened, she was very upset and angry. The goddess's close companions, Jaya and Vijaya, told her that as Nandi was one of Shiva's close followers, he would never do anything to displease him. 'So we should also have someone whom we can trust and who will obey us alone,' they said.

Parvati thought the matter over and then she went about making a beautiful boy with the dirt that she rubbed off her body. When she was done, she blew

softly on him, bringing him to life. She decided to call the little boy Ganesha. He would be her special son as well as her dedicated guard.

'You will be the gatekeeper, my dear—don't allow anybody in without my permission,' said Parvati with a smile, knowing that she would no longer have to depend on her husband's loyal gatekeeper, Nandi.

CHAPTER FIVE

A QUARREL WITH GANESHA

So the next time Shiva appeared at the door with his rowdy bunch, Ganesha refused to open the gate. The more Shiva insisted, the more stubbornly Ganesha shook his head in a stern 'No'.

Soon, there was a big commotion as Shiva left in a huff. Nandi was furious at this young boy's disrespectful attitude towards his lord and walked over to Parvati's gate and began to threaten Ganesha. However, Ganesha was brave, and despite Nandi's best efforts, he refused to budge. The other *ganas* were in a fix. They were amused

at Nandi's failure, enraged at Ganesha's audacity and afraid of Shiva's anger all at the same time.

Nandi and the other *gana*s went back to Shiva only to be rebuked by him. Nandi was pulled up by Shiva

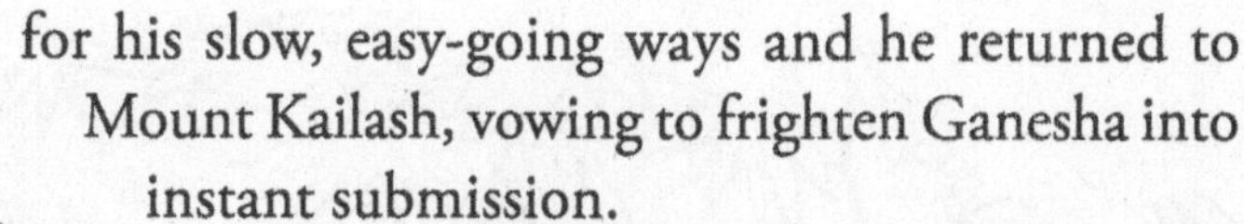

for his slow, easy-going ways and he returned to Mount Kailash, vowing to frighten Ganesha into instant submission.

He moved towards Ganesha menacingly. However, Ganesha was not one to be bullied and he brandished his club threateningly at Nandi and the rest of the *gana*s, frightening them out of their wits. They ran away leaving only Nandi behind to face Ganesha.

Nandi started attacking Ganesha with his horns. However, this child of Parvati was far too strong for him and he thrashed Nandi with his bare hands. When the other gods arrived to watch the contest, Ganesha scared them all away.

Shiva was enraged when he saw his *gana*s so badly treated, and he took out his mighty trident. Fearless, Ganesha challenged him to a duel and an angry Shiva cut off the boy's head with his all-powerful weapon.

Parvati's sorrow was great and deep, and she demanded that Shiva restore her son's head. She was also very angry and the gods asked her to show mercy

for they were afraid that she would destroy everything in her fury. She agreed to pardon them only on the condition that Ganesha would be brought back to life. She also demanded that he would be foremost in the line of worship and would receive prayer offerings before all the other gods.

However, unfortunately, Ganesha's lost head just could not be found. Shiva advised Nandi to go north. 'Go quickly. You must bring back the head of the first living creature you see and then fix it onto Ganesha's neck.'

Led by Nandi, the *ganas* rushed off at once. But all they found was the white elephant, Airavata, who was in fact Indra's mount. Remembering Shiva's command, they realized they had no choice—they cut off Airavata's head and fixed it on Ganesha's neck. This is how Ganesha acquired the head of an elephant and became the first god to receive offerings during any religious ceremony. Airavata's head was also restored because he was an immortal being. Thus, peace was restored to the heavenly abode and Ganesha became a part of the family, as well as a faithful follower of Lord Shiva.

One evening soon after, Shiva and Parvati were engaged in a fierce game of dice. Nandi agreed to be the referee. He was known for his fairness and would make sure that the game was judged impartially. It was up to him to also declare the winner.

However, this was a task Nandi dreaded as he did not know whom to please. Finally, when the closely fought game was over, Nandi, after some hesitation, declared Shiva the winner.

A furious Parvati refused to accept Nandi's verdict. 'You have been blatantly partial, O Divine Bull,' she said. 'It's obvious to anyone who has seen this game that you have been biased. As you have judged unfairly, I shall curse you in return. You will die due to an incurable disease. And, mark my words, for they always come true.'

Saying this, Parvati prepared to march off to her quarters, but Nandi wouldn't let her go. He was frightened by her terrible curse and knew of the agonies that such curses could inflict. Nandi blocked her path and looked at her beseechingly. He pleaded with her to take back her words.

'I do humbly beg your forgiveness, O Great Goddess,' said Nandi as he bowed and begged for mercy. 'But please understand my predicament. I have served the great god Shiva for many years now. He is dearer to me than any other. As a loyal servant, I cannot bear to see him lose. I made the wrong decision, but it was only because I adore him completely. I did it all to please him and in doing that, I have angered you. Please forgive me.'

He stood weeping profusely before Parvati till she felt pity for him. 'Very well, I understand what you are saying,' she said. 'But you still have to repent. During the monsoon season, every human worships Ganesha and celebrates a festival in his honour. During this time, they offer him all the things that they desire the most. From now on, you must also worship him during that time of the year and offer my son that which you covet the most.'

Nandi nodded. He thought of the fresh green grass which he enjoyed more than anything else in the world. He sighed at the thought of giving it up, but he had no choice. Following Parvati's demands, every monsoon, he worshipped Ganesha, offering him whole vessels of fresh green grass. Pleased to see her favourite son respected in this manner, Parvati forgave Nandi and took back her terrible curse. Thus all was right again and Nandi resumed his position as the loyal protector of Shiva and his family.

CHAPTER SIX

AN ENCOUNTER WITH THE GOD OF DEATH

Nandi was also a mighty warrior who fought many battles along with Shiva—and for many reasons. One such fabled contest became a matter of life and death in a way none other had.

There was once a priest named Shveta. He was a friend of the great sage Goutama and had a hermitage on the banks of the Ganga. Shveta was also very devoted to Shiva. When Shveta died, Yama sent his messengers to take Shveta to *naraka*—the Land of the Dead—but they were unable to enter the deceased sage's house.

When Yama realized his messengers were taking longer than usual, he sent his assistant Mrityu or Death to find out what had happened. When Mrityu arrived, he found Yama's messengers still standing outside Shveta's house, unable to enter. Shiva himself stood guard over the sage's body.

Nandi asked Mrityu, 'Why have you come here? What do you want?'

'I have come to take Shveta's soul to Yama,' replied Mrityu, 'His time on earth is up.'

Saying this, Mrityu quickly flung a lasso over Shveta's body to pull it towards him. Almost immediately, one of Shiva's companions struck Mrityu a hard blow and knocked him unconscious.

When this news reached Yama, he was furious. Bringing together all his companions, he attacked Shveta's house. Nandi and several of Shiva's followers, including Ganesha and Kartikeya, came face to face with Yama's army and a furious battle raged.

All the gods arrived on the scene, hoping to stop the terrible fight. But things only got worse. Yama was killed in combat. A solution had to be found immediately or the entire balance between Life and Death would be forever destroyed.

It was difficult to judge who was at fault as Yama was performing his duty, while Shiva was protecting his devotees. He was adamant that his devotees could not be taken away by the God of Death to *naraka* and they should, instead, go straight to Heaven.

Finally, in order to keep the peace, Shiva agreed to restore Yama's life. Nandi went and fetched water from the holy river Ganga and sprinkled it over Yama and others who had perished in the battle. At once, all of them returned to life. In return, Yama agreed to Shiva's demands and Shveta's soul went to Heaven.

Of course, this was neither the first nor the last time that Nandi fought for Lord Shiva.

CHAPTER SEVEN

NANDI FIGHTS A POWERFUL DEMON

Nandi's life continued to be entwined with Shiva's. Nandi was nearly always entangled in the conflicts and adventures of his lord.

Once the no-good and all-powerful demon Andhaka came to Mount Kailash while Shiva was away. He caught a single glimpse of Parvati and instantly fell in love with her. Right then, he decided that he would marry the goddess at any cost.

The sage Prahlada, who happened to be with Andhaka at that time, did his best to talk sense into him. 'You are out of your mind,' said Prahlada. 'She is Parvati, the Mother Goddess and the wife of Shiva. How can you even think of such a terrible thing? You will surely perish.'

His advice fell on deaf ears as Andhaka had already decided to take Parvati away by force. However, Shiva had left Nandi behind to protect Parvati and he defended her stoutly, attacking Andhaka with his trident and driving the demon back from the gates of Shiva's home. However, Andhaka was very strong and knocked Nandi unconscious with a heavy blow of his club.

Then Parvati took on her Shatarupa—the hundred-form avatar—where each of her forms looked exactly like the other. This confused Andhaka no end. He went around in maddening circles as he tried to figure out and catch the real Parvati, but failed.

Exhausted from all his efforts, Andhaka was easily struck down by a blow from the goddess's weapon. When the *asura* came to his senses, he found that Parvati had disappeared and Andhaka also quickly retreated to his own kingdom.

However, this defeat did little to change Andhaka's obsession. He called all his demon subjects and offered a huge reward to anyone who could bring Parvati to him. Yet again, Prahlada tried to dissuade Andhaka. This time, he told him the shocking secret about his birth.

'Shiva is actually your father,' he began. 'The demon Hiranyaksha had no son and he prayed to Shiva for a long

time to be blessed with a child. Shiva was pleased with his devotion, and appeared before Hiranyaksha. When he heard his request, Shiva narrated a story to Hiranyaksha; "This was a time when I was deep in meditation and Parvati, my wife, came up from behind and covered my eyes with her hands. Her palms were clammy and a drop of that sweat fell into the ground. From this darkness and perspiration came forth a fierce creature, who was our son. He is now called Andhaka. Take him and bring him up as your own," he said. "However, I will kill him myself if he goes against *dharma*—the rules that lay down what is right and what is wrong—or commits any evil." With this Shiva blessed him and gave him Andhaka to raise as his son. Thus Hiranyaksha obtained you for a son, and your true father and mother are Shiva and Parvati,' concluded Prahlada.

The story had little effect on Andhaka. Blinded by his desire to make Parvati his wife, he continued with his nefarious plans.

One day, when Shiva was away, Andhaka reached Mount Kailash, thinking that the moment was just right for abducting Parvati. But, once again, his path was blocked by Nandi, the ever-faithful gatekeeper, who was standing guard at the entrance. The two came to blows, for Nandi refused to let Andhaka pass. His trident struck Andhaka on the chest, and this made him very angry.

This altercation turned into a full-fledged battle. Andhaka came with a band of *asura*s and Nandi called upon Shiva's other *gana*s to fight them. However, Andhaka was very strong and his brigade of *asura*s finally defeated Nandi's army.

Although Nandi was very strong and fought and vanquished many of the *asuras*, he was finally overcome by the sheer number of opponents on Andhaka's side. Rendered helpless, as a last resort, Nandi turned to Lord Vishnu and prayed to him for help.

Lord Vishnu heard his plea and created an army of gods who charged into the battlefield and killed most of the *asuras* in no time. Andhaka, alarmed at the turn of events, fled in order to save his own skin.

Twelve years passed before Shiva returned and learnt of what had happened. In this period, Andhaka too had recovered from his injuries and humiliation, and he returned, more determined than ever to take Parvati away for sure. This time both Shiva and Vishnu fought against Andhaka and his army.

The two armies clashed with a thunderous roar that echoed across the universe. Shiva went into battle riding on Nandi. All the gods assembled in Heaven to witness this fierce struggle between good and evil.

The demon Danda, one of Andhaka's followers, fought with Ganesha. Kartikeya, yet another of Shiva's sons killed a demon called Hasti.

Nandi charged into the fray and attacked and killed all the *asuras* who came in his path. He fought fearlessly and easily gored the demons before they had time to react. Finally, he came face to face with Duryodhana, the general of the *asuras*, and after a protracted battle, defeated and killed him.

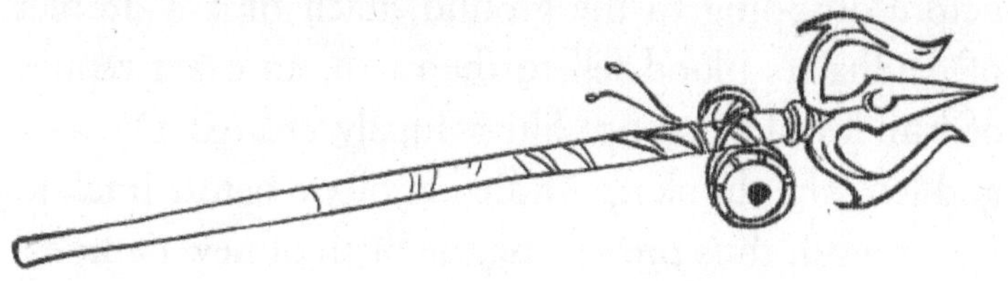

Saddened to see so many of his brethren being killed, Andhaka turned to his guru Shukracharya. This guru of the *asuras*, was an expert in the art of *sanjeevani*. It was a skill that could bring the dead back to life, and so he used this knowledge to rejuvenate all the demons who had been killed by Shiva's army.

Shiva then turned to Nandi and declared in a voice that brooked no disobedience, 'This can't go on. We have to do something about Shukracharya, else we will lose this battle. You must bring Shukracharya to me.'

Nandi charged his way through the entire *asura* camp, knocking down all who came in his path. Shukracharya was guarded by several fierce demons. However, Nandi was fearless and he gored all the powerful *asuras* to death in a swift motion. Then, he captured Shukracharya and brought him back to Shiva. The mighty god opened his mouth till it was as wide as a cave and swallowed Shukracharya, thus imprisoning him in his stomach.

With the *asura* guru out of the way, the gods began to win again and all the demons were defeated, except Andhaka himself. All the weapons of the gods only grazed his skin, merely creating minor wounds before dropping to the ground. Each time a droplet of Andhaka's blood fell to the earth, an exact replica of him would rise up. Shiva finally created Devi—a goddess who drank up Andhaka's blood before it fell to the ground, thus preventing the birth of new demons.

The war went on for two thousand and eight hundred years. At long last, Andhaka and Shiva met face to face, and the demon charged towards him with a club. Vishnu turned to Shiva and instructed him in low, urgent tones. 'You must kill the demon inside Andhaka and free the man.'

Shiva picked up his trident and pierced Andhaka's heart with it. The demon in turn struck Shiva with a club. The blow bounced off harmlessly and only angered Shiva more, and he drove the trident even further into Andhaka's body. He raised his trident to the sky with the body of the *asura* stuck to one prong. The fire that blazed forth from Shiva's eyes dried up Andhaka's blood.

The *asura* was held aloft in this manner for a thousand years, until his flesh fell away and only his skin and bones were left behind. As Andhaka lay there poised on the point of the trident, the evil left him and all his sins were forgiven. He started to pray to Shiva, pleading for a boon so that he could devote his new life to the Lord.

Shiva granted his boon, freed Andhaka from the trident and cleaned his wounds. The battle over, Shukracharya prayed to Shiva and was finally released from his stomach.

As Andhaka was no longer an *asura*, he was renamed Bhringi and became one of Shiva's loyal *ganapatis*. Whenever Shiva did the *tandava*, he was accompanied by both Nandi and Bhringi. He became a favoured follower of Shiva, second only to Nandi.

CHAPTER EIGHT

THE ETERNAL DEVOTEE

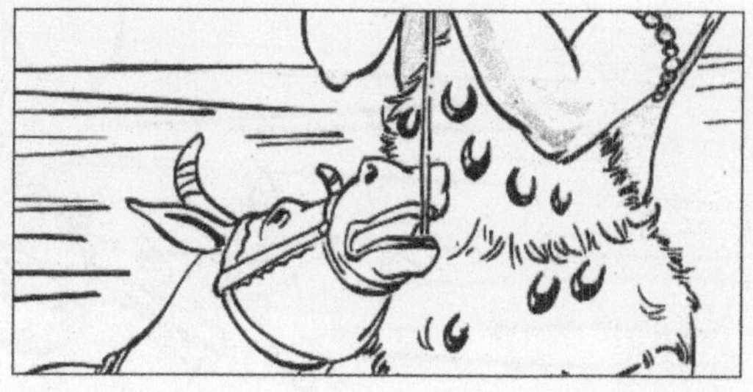

Nandi was also witness to the *samudra manthan*—when the Ocean was being churned for the nectar or *amrit* that had the powers to grant immortality. The gods and the *asuras* held either end of the serpent Vasuki as the rope that was wrapped around Mount Meru to churn the waters.

The churning set off a great tumult in the Ocean. The waters rose terribly high and gave off an ominous roar. The bubbling ocean emitted the poisonous liquid called Halahala. Its pungent fumes brought tears to the eyes

of even those who were watching from afar. The poison spread quickly all over the Ocean, turning it black, and the sticky liquid threatened to trap anyone caught in its path. Both the gods and the *asura*s fled in fear.

Finally, it was Shiva who came to their rescue. He arrived on the scene, riding his faithful companion Nandi. Shiva dismounted and cupped the rapidly spreading poison in the palms of his hands, which grew large enough to hold the entire Ocean. He drank the poison steadily without flinching. He also knew he would have to hold the poison securely in his throat, and Parvati placed her hand on his throat to help him. Shiva's throat turned blue and thus he came to be known as Neelakantha, the blue-throated one, as well as Vishakantha, the one who holds poison in his throat.

As he scooped up the poison, some drops spilled onto the ocean floor and Nandi quickly went over and licked it up before it could do any more damage. The gods were horrified, but Shiva drove away their fears, saying, 'Nandi is my most loyal disciple. He has immersed himself in me so completely that no harm can ever befall him. He has imbibed my powers and I will always protect him.' And thus Nandi's eternal devotion to his Lord was well rewarded.

Nandi continued to follow Shiva through his journeys across Heaven and earth, helping him in his time of need and playing a crucial role in events that changed the course of history.

CHAPTER NINE

NANDI'S CURSE

Whenever the need arose, Nandi would rise to battle with ferocity, but generally he was mild by nature. However, when provoked, he could be fierce.

No wonder then that he played a part in an event that foreshadowed one of the greatest battles—the one between Rama and Ravana.

Kuber, who was the God of Wealth and also Ravana's elder brother had a fine chariot called the Pushpak Vimana that flew high into the air. Having stolen it from his brother, Ravana flew around the entire universe on the magnificent chariot. Finally, he arrived at Mount

Kailash and demanded to see Shiva. However, Nandi, the faithful gatekeeper, refused him entry.

'No one can enter his premises just like that—people undertake penance and pray for centuries before Lord Shiva graces them with an appearance,' he explained patiently.

Ravana was furious. He replied haughtily, 'Do you know who I am? I am the King of the *Rakshasa*s and the Lord of Lanka. I've defeated most kings.

Even the most powerful of gods are scared of me.'

Despite such strong words, Nandi refused to budge from his place.

Ravana changed his tactics and began to mock him. He said, 'You think you can stop me? Why you hardly look like a bull. In fact, I think you are more like a monkey.'

Nandi, angered by Ravana's unforgivable rudeness, reared his head up, snorted and said, 'You, who are so arrogant, will pay the price for your words. One day, you will be defeated by the very same monkeys that you have insulted right now.'

And indeed Nandi's curse came true later. Lanka—Ravana's kingdom—was set on fire by Hanuman, the divine *vanara* or monkey, when he went in search of Sita who had been abducted and forcibly taken to Lanka by Ravana.

Hanuman was also a devotee of Shiva and it was Nandi who taught him the sacred hymns of Shiva for prayer. He also gave him lessons in humility, which a creature of great strength needed to possess in abundant measure to be truly great. And who would know this better than Nandi, the ever-obedient and loyal devotee of Lord Shiva!

MythNotes

In ancient times, the bull was worshipped because people lived off the land and had large herds of bulls, cows and oxen to plough their fields. Nandi is regarded as the guardian deity of all kinds of cattle. Once, it is said, Shiva told Nandi to deliver a message to his devotees on earth, but Nandi accidentally delivered the wrong message. As a result, the furious god punished him by ordering Nandi to stay on earth and help the farmers plough their fields. The festival of Mattu Pongal held in Tamil Nadu in the month of January celebrates Nandi and his descendants who continue to help people in farming.

An idol of Nandi is found in nearly all Shiva temples. The bull seated in front also denotes the gatekeeper and no temple is complete without the gentle guardianship of Nandi.

The Nandi temple in Basavanagudi, Karnataka, has a giant Nandi statue. The story recounts how a rampaging bull was clubbed by a farmer and it immediately turned to stone. The terrified farmers realized that they had offended a divine being and built a temple around the statue. But the bull kept growing. The farmers then prayed to Shiva, who helped them and curbed the stone bull from growing any larger.

The Sri Masilamaneeswarar temple in Thirumullaivayil, Tamil Nadu, is home to a large Nandi statue that was built to commemorate the ancient king Thondaimaan's victory against two demon brothers with the help of Nandi.